The Gingerbread Man

Contents

The Gingerbread Man
A traditional tale — 2

Gingerbread Is Fun to Make
A poem — 21

Gingerbread People
A recipe — 22

Hungry Fox
A picture story to tell — 24

Great Escape!
A map — 26

Ginger
A report — 28

Our Weekend
A recount — 30

Think and Link
Questions to discuss — 32

Once upon a time,
an old man and an old woman
were sitting in their kitchen.
They were both feeling hungry.
They wanted a snack.

"Let's make some gingerbread,"
said the woman.

"Yum! I love gingerbread!"
replied the man.

Quickly, they found everything they needed. They measured and poured. They stirred and mixed and rolled.

Then the woman cut out
a big gingerbread man.

"He can have raisins for his eyes
and a cherry for his nose," she said.

"And some orange rind
for his mouth," said the man.

Before long, the delicious smell of gingerbread filled the kitchen. But as soon as the man and the woman opened the oven door, the gingerbread man jumped out and ran away.

"Stop! Stop! We're hungry!"
shouted the man.

"Stop! Stop! We do love gingerbread!"
cried the woman.

The man and the woman
ran after the gingerbread man,
but he just ran faster.

"Run, run, as fast as you can.
You can't catch me –
I'm the gingerbread man."

He ran past a tree, where a boy was pushing a girl on a swing.

"Stop! Stop!" shouted the girl.

"We love gingerbread!" called the boy.

The man and the woman and the boy and the girl all ran after the gingerbread man, but he just ran faster.

"Run, run, as fast as you can.
You can't catch me –
I'm the gingerbread man."

He ran and ran, past a dog and a cat and on through the town.

"Stop! Stop!" meowed the cat.

"We love gingerbread!" barked the dog.

The gingerbread man kept running. Soon he had left the town far behind.

"Run, run, as fast as you can.
You can't catch me –
I'm the gingerbread man."

He ran up a hill, and everyone ran after him. He ran down the other side, and everyone got closer.

Then the gingerbread man came to a river. He stopped and stared.

"What can I do? There is no bridge!" cried the gingerbread man.

Suddenly, a fox appeared from behind a tree.
"Don't worry, little gingerbread man. Just hop on my back and I'll carry you across," said the fox.

The gingerbread man held on tightly as the fox jumped into the water. But soon...

"Help! My feet are getting wet!" called the gingerbread man.

"Climb up on my head and you'll keep dry," said the fox.

But in no time at all
his feet were getting wet again.

"Help! My feet are getting wet!"
shouted the gingerbread man.

"Climb out on my nose
and you'll keep dry," said the fox.

"Thank you!"
said the gingerbread man,
as he climbed out
on the fox's nose.

"Thank *you*!" said the fox, as he swallowed the gingerbread man and licked his lips.
"I love gingerbread, too!"

Gingerbread Is Fun to Make

Gingerbread is fun to make,
It's sweet and brown and yummy.
When you put it in your mouth,
It ends up in your tummy.

Chorus:

*Gingerbread is fun to make.
Gingerbread is yummy.
Never let it run away,
Just put it in your tummy.*

Gingerbread is fun to make,
You stir and mix and beat it.
But if you let it run away,
You'll never get to eat it!

Poem can be sung to the tune of "Yankee Doodle"
or "This Is the Way We Wash Our Clothes"

Use this recipe to have some fun.
Then you can decorate what you've done.

Gingerbread People

What you need:

- half a cup of brown sugar
- one cup of butter (or margarine)
- half a cup of honey
- one egg
- a pinch of salt
- two and a half cups of flour
- four teaspoons of ground ginger
- one teaspoon of cinnamon
- half a teaspoon of baking soda

What you do:

1. Mix the sugar and the butter in a bowl. Then beat in the honey and the egg.

2. Mix the rest of the ingredients. Slowly add them to the butter mixture to make a dough.

3. Roll out the dough on a lightly floured surface. Cut out your gingerbread people.

4. Place your gingerbread people on a greased baking sheet. Add some decorations if you wish. Bake for 10–12 minutes at 160°C (325°F).

5. Let your gingerbread people cool and finish decorating them. Now eat them!

What other gingerbread shapes can you make? How would you decorate them?

Is Fox the "bad guy" according to you?
Let's look at that morning from his point of view.

Hungry Fox

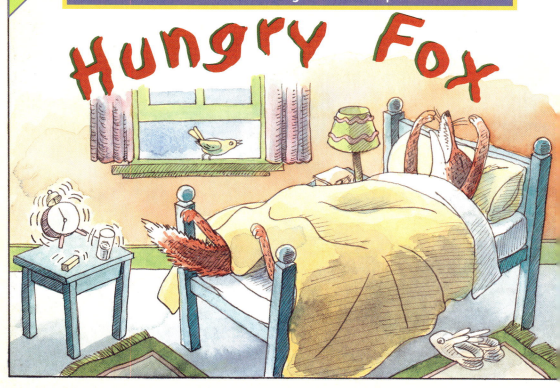

What could the other characters have been doing on the morning of the story?

25

Great Escape!

The gingerbread man looks far and wide.
Where can he run to? Where can he hide?

The smell is a treat and the taste is nice.
Ginger is all you could want from a spice.

Ginger

What Is Ginger?

Ginger is a spice that comes from the ginger plant. It has a strong taste and smell. The ginger we use comes from the part of the stem that grows along the ground. This special stem is called a *rhizome*.

The Ginger Plant

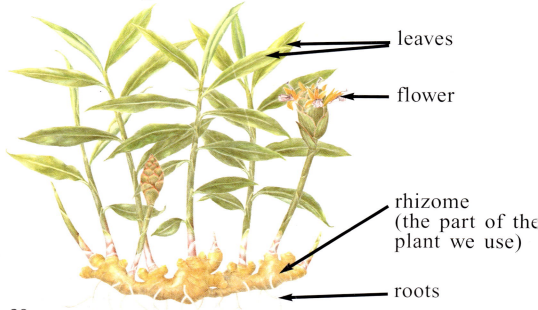

leaves

flower

rhizome (the part of the plant we use)

roots

Ginger in Action!

ground ginger

crystallized ginger

pickled ginger

> When something interesting happens to you, writing about it is a fun thing to do!

Our Weekend
By Carl and Katie

On Saturday the most amazing thing happened. We were playing on the swing when we saw a gingerbread man run past. We couldn't believe our eyes!

"Stop, stop!" we shouted,
but the gingerbread man didn't stop.
Just then a man and a woman appeared
They were chasing the gingerbread man

We started running with them.
We ran as fast as we could.
It was very tiring. When we ran through the town, a cat and a dog started chasing the gingerbread man, too.

At last we came to a river. We thought the gingerbread man was trapped, but he wasn't! A fox came and started to give him a ride across the river. Then, suddenly, the fox ate him.

What a very strange day!

Think and Link

Poem and Story

Do you think it is better to say the poem or to sing it? Why?

What parts of the story could you sing? What tune would you use?

Story and Recipe

Which things are the same on pages 4 and 22? Which are different?

What do you think might have happened if the woman in the story had made lots of gingerbread people?

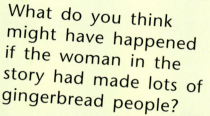

Story and Hungry Fox

Which characters wanted to eat the gingerbread man? Why do you think they wanted to eat him? If they were hungry, what else could they have done?

Story and Map

Which places and characters can you find in both the story and the map?

Why do you think the map includes more places and more characters?

Telling Stories

How do pages 24 and 25 tell a story? How is this different from the way pages 2 to 20 tell a story? Do any other parts of the book tell a story? How do they do this?